I0177540

Placing Your Order

(Steps for Creating Successful Manifestations)

K.C. Craig

K.C. Craig

Copyright © 2007 by K.C. Craig
All Right Reserved.

Published by
RMS Publications Company
Beverly Hills, California

All the characters in this book are fictious and any resemblance to actual persons, living or dead, is purely coincidental. No part of this publication may be reproduced, stored in a retrieval system, or transmitted, in any form or by any means, electronic, mechanical, photocopying, recording or otherwise without the prior written permission of RMS Publications Company.

Cover by Andrey Pustovoy

Library of Congress Catalog Card Number:
Available from the Publisher.

ISBN 9781882373109

Printed in the United States of America

To my beloved **Richard:**
my **husband,** my **partner,** my **friend**
along life's journey

Contents

Acknowledgements

God, the Source of All Being: Thank You for Your loving hand in mine as I wrote Your book. What can I say but "Thank You, thank You, thank You for the honor and privilege of being of service to You and humanity in helping others to help themselves, for the highest good and greatest joy for all. Here is my prayer to you:

"Thank You, God, for this beautiful, glorious day. And, thank You, God, for having me to be a part of it. Today, I would do Your work. Take my hands, my head, my heart, and let them be channels through which Your work is done. Let my voice serve You. May I be a reflection of Your Love and Light, and a blessing for those in need. Amen."

Ernest Holmes: As my spiritual mentor, you empowered my soul by giving my spirit wings to fly.

Mama and Daddy: In life, we all are given a special gift from God. You were mine.

Richard: Your unconditional love and support makes me happy with every breath I take.

My Big Sis, Patty (Seel): I am forever grateful because you are both the best sister in the world AND my best friend. How did I get so blessed?

Alicia (Pollock): You are my spiritual heart…sharing without filtering. What a gift!

Diane (Pressman): You have taught me the true meaning of lasting friendship.

Jimmy (Wagner): You make my heart laugh, always. Your support with "Inner Channels" helped me understand that true giving is always "gratis."

Jeffrey (Starr): You and me and FAU...you had me at hello! Thank you, cherished friend, for teaching me the importance of being true to yourself.

Paula (Pines): Your persevering spirit and adventurous heart inspire me.

Bobby (Barzler):You'll always have a piece of my heart.

Judy (Hoban) and Joan (Vernotzy) (or should I say Joan and Judy?): Your love and support set me upon my path.

Gary Chapman, *"Anything's Possible,"* and R. Kelly, *"I Believe I Can Fly,"*: Your music helped lift me to the realm of absolute belief.

Charles Suniga: Listening to your album, *"Moments of Peace: The Journey"* created a magical and mystical, vibrational atmosphere during my meditations.

Linda Hart Michels: Thank you for the gift of realizing I can set boundaries.

Mark Torgenson: Thank you for your Transformational Music of my heart's desire.

Danielle, Susan, and Adam at Starbucks in the PanAm Shopping Center: Who knew you would provide me with such a creative atmosphere every Saturday at 6 am?!

And, especially, to all my friends: I am who I am because of you!

PREFACE

My motive in writing this book is to help others to help themselves through the power of thought and self-manifestation, for the highest good and greatest joy for all. I want to share my experiences and "my truth" in manifesting by sharing my beliefs that have contributed to my understanding of self-manifestation.

What do I mean when I say "manifesting"? It is not an 'instant' materialization of what I want, although I do believe at some point in mankind's development, this will be as normal as breathing...but that's a long way down the road. For now, mankind is in the learning process: to use the power of its thoughts to bring into existence that which it desires. Once our thought is made, it goes out into the Universe and returns to us somewhere down the line, in all its perfection. It is making its way to us as we are making our way to it, until, with God's perfect timing, we meet with our desire on this physical plane of existence.

One day while reading *Love and Law* by Ernest Holmes, I had what is normally referred to as my "*aha*" moment. It was as if that proverbial light bulb went off for me and my life changed forever. How? I realized that I had the power to control my thoughts, and in doing so, I had the power over what I wanted to have, to do, and to become.

But having this knowledge didn't mean I was always successful in manifesting my heart's desires. One day I sat down and tried to figure out why my most successful manifestations became a reality....from thought to physical form. Suddenly, I started writing down a very simple equation, and in that instance came such clarity that I knew I would be writing a book to share my experiences in manifesting and to give you this basic equation:

$$(I + Mo) + D^I + B = M$$

Don't panic! It only means:

Intent+Motive+Intensity of Desire+Belief = Manifestation

I thought over and over again just which part of my equation was the most important. I can give you reasons why each one is the vital piece. In actuality, if any of these parts is missing, so will your manifestation be... missing!

I'm going to discuss each part of the equation and show not how important each part is, but how all parts come together and flow into perfect manifestation.

There have been so many others who have written so much more eloquently and extensively on this concept than I could ever do. Yet, I felt compelled to share my knowledge and experiences with others; my successes as well as my failures in manifesting. Throughout this book I make reference to my own experiences because it is important for you to see how my experiences have molded my belief in this process of manifestation. It is my truth, resonating within my heart.

You'll note this is just a simple, little book. I'm hoping my contributions are to help you structure your thoughts, and provide you with the steps that lead to a successful manifestation, in a clear, concise, and simple manner— this is a primer so to speak—so that regardless of race, creed, color, education, money, or power, anyone reading this book can truly understand this concept of manifestation and take back the power of control over their lives.

With God, all things are possible. And so, I find myself writing a book on manifestation. Actually, I would rather have my fingernails AND toenails pulled out slowly, very slowly, than to have to write a book. But, to have such knowledge and not to share it with those who are ready to read about manifesting and bring it into their daily lives would go against my deepest belief of helping others to help themselves. What better way to help someone to help himself than to show him how to manifest his wants, needs, and desires on his current plane of existence, here on planet Earth.

In the writing of this book, I have asked myself so very often, how can I help someone change his thoughts about himself and his life, his want or his lack, when everyday is a struggle just to put food on the table, a roof over his head, and the clothes on his back? When all he sees is lack and struggle, how can I help another soul find this truth of manifestation and help him to believe he can do what is his God-given right to do? Quite honestly, I have no idea. What I do know, however, is that by example and by sharing this book, I hope to perhaps open his mind to the possibility that he CAN manifest. After all, this is the whole purpose of this book, to help others to help themselves through the power of their thoughts to take back control of their lives through the power of manifestation. Everyone must start somewhere. For now, it's just important that I share my truth and what I've learned with others, hoping to inspire a spark within them for further discovery and perhaps to use this information as their first steps along their path of self-discovery and self manifestation.

For those of you who are already on a conscious or subconscious level to understand self-manifestation, since you've picked up this book, I know you will be able to understand the equation and use it, and then run with it...all the way to your heart's desires.

Here's hoping you, too, have your "*aha*" moment. Now, let's go and have some fun in learning to manifest our heart's desires.

Blessings from my heart to yours!

K.C. Craig
May 17, 2007

Okay, God, here we go:
Arm-in-arm, hand-in-hand.
I wonder what wonderful, positive, fun,
Glorious adventures await me today?!

I wonder who will I meet?
What will I learn and what will I teach?
Who will I help and who will help me?

K.C. Craig

THE BACKSTORY
(Why it Works!)

We are powerful. We are powerful because our thoughts are powerful. Our thoughts are powerful because they manifest EVERYTHING we see, hear, taste, touch, and smell...EVERYTHING we are or ever will be... EVERYTHING we do or ever will do...and thoughts manifest EVERYTHING we have or ever will have on this physical plane of existence. Our thoughts create all in our lives: good, bad, or boring!

Pretty awesome statements, aren't they? You bet, but then, the Universe IS awesome!

Our thoughts make seen what is unseen on this plane of physical existence. This unseen energy is just waiting to come into physical form. Everything is already 'out there.' We're just bringing it into the level of vibratory energy of this physical world. In manifesting, we are placing our order with the Universal Mind and yes, the moment we do so, the thought has actually 'manifested' that desire. We are just waiting for it to come to us just as we are going towards it. How, when, where is NOT up to us...it is best to leave the fine tuning up to the Universe.

We'll learn later on why it's better for the Universe to take the ball and run with it.

How is this possible? What are my thoughts made of? Just who or what is filling my order, and where am I placing my order for manifestation? How is it filled? How do my thoughts come back to me as a physical manifestation?

Well, hold onto your hats, because you're in for a fun and thrilling ride from the Universe... here's the long and the short of it....the backstory.

God

God is a good place to start because God is always a good place to start (anything). It all begins with the concept of God and our relationship to God. Let's start with the use of the word "God." There is, in truth, only One Source, and it is from this Source that all being is, including you and me. I could have just as easily used the word Allah, Krishna, Universal Mind, Universal Spirit, Universal Intelligence, Universal Creativity or one of many other names by which the One Source of All Being is known. It doesn't really matter...just choose whatever word vibrates within you and brings your soul to its place of ultimate knowing and understanding. I'll be using"God" or "pronouns "He or She, Him or Her" interchangeably rather than using the pronoun "It." Being a human being, this usage helps me to identify personally with my relationship with God.

God in Us

Just what is our relationship to God? I think the phrase "We are made in the image of God" does not refer to our physical being, but rather to our vibrational energy of Cosmic Consciousness. God is the One Source of all Being. So then surely, we must be some part of God made manifest. But what part? We are a part of His consciousness made manifest. Why? We are used as an avenue of Her expression of creativity on this physical plane of existence. Think of yourself as a part of God individualized. Since the Universe is always in the process of becoming something else [Remember the old adage, "The only constant in the Universe is change"], it makes sense that through us, God is also becoming, growing, and changing into a more complete expression of what He is. Think of yourself as the "process" of God becoming and not the perfection She already is.

Do you remember the equation:
If $A = B$, and $B = C$, then $A = C$? I've applied this to my belief that I am a creative part of God as follows:

A = God is the creative force in the Universe, which creates all living things;

B = God has empowered all living things with the power to create;

17

C = Therefore, as a living, created being, I have the power to create.

But just how do I create? What tools do I have at my disposal? These are the questions upon which the entire concept of manifestation is based.

God's Gifts to Mankind

God is so cool. He has given us mere mortals two incredible gifts (or tools) so that we may create our heart's desires right here, right now:

1) the power of our thoughts through the use of the Universal Law of Cause and Effect; and

2) free will using the spiritual Law of Attraction.

Let's first discuss what our thoughts are and then how we use them through free will to create what we want.

Thoughts

What are thoughts? Everything in the Universe is made up of varying vibrating rates of energy. Want a shocker? The only difference between you and chair you're sitting in is the rate of vibration and how that energy vibration is organized!

The latest theory put out by physicists is called Quantum Theory, which states that everything in the Universe is made up of packets of vibrating energy. Every choice is a qualitative choice...only one of many possible choices, which in turn, brings about every possible world. It is in our choosing of that one specific possibility that makes itself manifest. I will not be discussing this theory in any greater detail, but, you must take this as truth or else you will not be able to understand just how powerful you are. It is the vibrational energy of our thoughts which are manifested on this physical plane of reality. And our choosing is done through our thoughts.

Your thoughts create all you are, all you have, and all you will ever become. "How is this possible?" you say to yourself, "I don't want to be poor, unhealthy, unhappy, or unloved." Yet, I bet if you look long and hard enough, you'll find that at some point in your life, you truly believed you were poor, unhealthy, unhappy, or unloved. And, you felt this way with great intensity. Often, these are feelings felt on our subconscious level, which makes it pretty difficult to even know we are having such thoughts! But it is important to trace where we came up with these negative thoughts about ourselves in order to use our ability to manifest correctly. Here are three instances where my thoughts created my reality of myself and my situations, in terms of health, wealth, and weight.

—

19

Health Thoughts

As a child, I had rheumatic fever. I was so sickly and always heard these phrases from my parents, "You're not a healthy person. You have to be careful. You can't play and run like the other children. We're afraid you'll die." I picked up their fear, as children normally do, about my health and it stayed with me in adulthood. Needless to say, for most of my life, I have always thought of myself as not a well person....and sure enough, I haven't been. It's been one illness after another.

In 1994, I was diagnosed with the Epstein Barr virus (a form of Chronic Fatigue Syndrome) and in 1998, I developed Fibromyalgia. Talk about pain and the feeling of desperation. I could barely move. It's really amazing how our thoughts attract to us exactly what we feel our reality is; for me, it was that I was an unhealthy person. I was told by my doctors that there was nothing they could do to help me and to get ready for a lifetime of pain killers. Even back then I firmly believed that we bring to ourselves situations we need for our growth, I felt this current situation was no different. I knew that what came out of this experience I would incorporate into my very being for future use in my life. My "work" through this situation was to figure out why I had brought ill health to myself. Once I realized to the very core of my being I had believed what my parents had ingrained in my when I was when I was a child of being sickly, (discussed later in the chapter on Belief). I kept repeating the mantra: "I am strong. I am healthy. I have energy, vitality, and stamina. I am healed." From morning to night, I would repeat this mantra until this feeling of health was part of my consciousness. Once it took hold there, I kept repeating and repeating it until that feeling of health became part of my subconscious. And it was at that moment when my thoughts had changed to thoughts of being healthy, I met, quite by accident (don't you just love synchronicity?) a wonderful healer who helped me release the situation that had been making me so ill because I was ready to accept the perfect health that was mine by Divine right. My thoughts were one of being completely and truly healed. This was the first proof I had of the power of my mind bringing to me exactly what I wanted and needed, and exactly what I believed to be true. While I occasionally have a relapse (as well all know life can be very stressful and our thoughts tend to wander, all I need to is to start "setting my thoughts strait" and by repeating my mantras, and health is mine once again.

Wealth Thoughts

When I was growing up, we were poor. Mama was a beautician and Daddy drove a taxi cab. It was very difficult to make ends meet, yet we always survived. Mom always said, "We'll just make it this month." So, I had this mentality that it's okay to be poor...I don't need wealth because I can always make ends meet. Sure enough, that's how my life has been up to now....living paycheck to paycheck. I had a roof over my head, food in my belly, clothes on my back, the utilities paid, but there was little money left for the "goodies" of life. In addition to this, I had always considered myself to be a nonmaterial person. Who needs money? My husband called me his "immaterial girl in a material world." I thought of myself this way, too, because, remember, I don't need wealth. After all, I'm a spiritual being...what do I need money for? But, in my quest for learning about manifesting, I hadn't realized how powerfully my thoughts about money and material goods had shaped my life. One day I realized that this was my mother's tape I had been playing in my head all these years. It had colored my thoughts and had shaped my relationship with money. What a relief to find out that by changing my thought from "I can always make ends meet," to "I am fabulously wealthy," I changed my reality of and experience with wealth. While this is still a work in progress, I know this to be true...I am making my way to fabulous wealth just as fabulous wealth is making its way to me. Abundance is mine, and I'm claiming it and accepting it as my Truth right now! We MUST change our thoughts in order to change our life into what we wish it to become.

Weight Thoughts

I've always considered myself as an overweight person with bouts of being slim. Talk about a struggle. For the last 14 years, I've dieted and dieted, losing 20 pounds, and then regaining it back, over and over again. Whenever I lost more than 20 pounds, I found ways to sabotage myself. This cycle continued until I started working on manifesting. In meditation one day, I could hear my grandmother, who was constantly put me down, say "You're fat and overweight. You keep busting the crotch out of your shorts." Needless to say, as a child of eight, I was devastated. But even more harmful than being demoralized was that I had allowed that incident to color how I viewed my body from then on. I can't tell you I was conscious of my feeling of being a "fat" person. But I can surely tell you I've done everything to make sure I have been one. Again, once I found the cause for my feeling, I decided that if I can manifest health and wealth, then I can surely manifest being the correct weight to feel good in my body. While coming up with the correct mantra for me on weight loss, a most remarkable thing happened. I had been having trouble figuring out just what the mantra should be. Obviously, the ones I'd had in the past hadn't worked. Rather than concentrating on weight loss, I turned my energy (thoughts) to a more positive mantra. Instead of trying to obtain an arbitrary weight number, I

---

now prefer to say: "I am healthy and feel comfortable in my body and my clothes." Short and sweet. Can you see the difference? I'm still a work in progress on this…I'll keep you posted. But I know that since it has become part of my belief system, it's a done deal.

I can't begin to tell you how much my thoughts have changed and so has my life since I realized that my thoughts about health, wealth, and weight belonged to someone else. I bring these issues up because many times we may not even be aware we are subconsciously playing tapes, which were ingrained into us when we were young…too young to realize our thoughts had already been shaped into manifesting certain realities we have been experiencing all our lives.

Now, I want to make one thing perfectly clear. Yes, you CAN manifest without knowing the "why" of your situation. I've done it before. But, I truly feel for health, wealth, and happiness, or anything else, you MUST find the underlying causes that have dictated your condition and lack so that situation doesn't reappear. If the condition reappears, it's probably because we haven't been as diligent as we should have been in controlling our thoughts. Finding our underlying cause does takes a lot of deep introspection, and this in itself can be painful to experience. But I can tell you it's well worth it not to have to keep manifesting over and over again the solution to the same issue, or not being able to manifest what you want at all. Why tire yourself out with re-manifesting? Put your thoughts to better use!

Legal Tender

God has given our thoughts such power that our thoughts are the legal tender of the Universe. It is with our thoughts that we "buy" what we want from the Universe's unlimited storehouse of abundance. Our thoughts can buy us all the goodies we can imagine or handle.

The Law of Cause and Effect

Just how do I use this powerful Universal legal tender of my thoughts in order to manifest my desires? It is done through The Universal Law of Cause of Effect. Just as in this physical world there are natural laws, which are in operation, so, too, there are natural laws in the non-seen world, which operate just as surely and just as naturally.

In essence, the Law of Cause and Effect states that our thoughts, a vibrating energy, goes out into the Universal Mind that creates what we desire and returns our desire to this plane of existence as a physical manifestation. Here's how it works:

1) We have a thought (based on a desire) which is referred to as the Cause;

2) This thought, this vibrating energy, goes out into the Universal Mind;

3) Universal Mind transforms our thought; and

4) It is returned to this physical plane of existence as the Effect or Manifestation.

Our thought is transformed through the use of a vibrational creative energy, which the Universal Mind uses for all that He creates. This vibrational energy is a part of Mind that He uses to transform His thoughts into material manifestations. And, as we learned, since God creates, then we, too, can create using this vibrating energy. Our thoughts are the **only** medium through which our order can be placed!

Here's the good part. You don't even have to go looking for Mind and this vibrational fabric. Why? Because Mind and this vibrational energy runs through us, is in us; we are a part of Mind just as Mind is a part of us; and so we only have to reach out with our thoughts and grab hold. When we do, our thoughts are immediately surrounded by this vibrational energy. I like to think of my thought as a mold of some sort (a specific desire). Let's use the thought of a brand new car. Then, think of this vibrational energy as a sponge which soaks up every one of our thought-molds. It squeezes out our thought-mold and that energy is now transformed into the physical manifestation: a beautiful, brand new car. This energy has always existed; it's just been molded (transformed) into the specific form of your thought (desire). It could have been molded into any object or feeling. Now, here is one of the most important concepts you need to understand. This energy is limitless energy and does not think in terms of limitations; nor can it give you anything but what your thoughts have given this energy to manifest. It is impersonal and neutral...good in/good out ...garbage in/garbage out. Think of this vibrating energy as a machine that can only produce from what materials (thoughts) are placed into it.

Are you aware that we all manifest on a daily basis? Why have a wasted thought? Since our minds are never at rest, and we are always thinking of this or that, why not use this Law to our benefit? We use it to our detriment all the time. It's time to take control over our lives. By now, I'm sure you're asking yourself, "Do I really have that much control over my life?" I know it's pretty frightening to think that our thoughts are the cause of our current situation in life. But, if I believe that my thoughts are powerful and whatever I think comes back to me manifested, then it behooves me to take control over my daily thoughts to ensure that I'm sending out only the positive and loving vibrations I want to manifest. This only happens through constant, daily practice. Be aware at all times exactly what your thoughts are. The minute you find yourself focusing on the negative, switch your thoughts to see how what you're focusing on can be considered positive. Or, come up with a mantra that snaps you out of the negativity. Just do whatever you need to do to change your thought energy to the positive. Instead of saying, "I am not sick," focus on the positive by saying, "I am well."

Remember this: Like most truths, the Law of Cause and Effect is simple, but also like most truths, it's their application we find difficult. So we must be ever controlling our thoughts and ever vigilant to express only for the highest good and greatest joy for all concerned. This takes lots and lots of practice! Practice, practice, and more practice, until manifesting the positive is as natural to you as breathing.

Free Will
Now God's second great gift to us, free will, comes into play. Not only does the Universe give us the power of our thoughts to manifest what we want, She gives us the choice of what we want to do with what we've manifested through our thoughts. Through the power of our choices in life, we create our own happiness or sorrow

If thoughts are the medium of manifestation, then free will is the mechanism to choose how we want to use our thoughts.

God has given us this tremendous privilege of choice, but with such a privilege comes the responsibility for our actions or choices, because as we've already learned, our thoughts create our life. For many, such a responsibility is a scary thought. This means the blame game is over! For me, free will is awesome because it gives me the power over my life, to create the reality of my life as I choose it to be.

The Law of Attraction
With our free will comes another spiritual Universal Law. It is the Law of Attraction which says "like attracts like" or "like thoughts attract the same like thoughts." Whatever you send out comes back to you just like you sent it out! Positive and loving thoughts create the same positive and loving thoughts, which are returned to you in ways unimaginable, just as creating negative and unloving thoughts create unimaginable negativity in your life. Whether intentionally or unintentionally, our thoughts go out into this energy and are "imprinted" on this Source of all creation. I now choose to be intentional with my thoughts so that I may become aligned and connected to this Universal Source, for the highest good

and greatest joy for all. Why not manifest perpetual good that not only helps me, but always helps others to help themselves as well?

We now know the power of our thoughts in manifesting our lives. If you have been able to get your mind wrapped around just how powerful your thoughts are and that you can create your heart's desire through your thoughts, then let's proceed with finding out how to structure an effective thought. In the upcoming chapters, we're going to discuss the components of a thought required for successful, positive, and loving manifestations…Intent, Motive, Desire, and Belief. It's fun to get what we ask for…we just need to know how to ask! And the question you should ask is "WHAT do I want?

Intent

(What do you want?)
Equation: I +

You can't manifest what you don't know you want. Identifying what it is you truly desire begins the process of placing your order with the Universe. Instead of focusing negatively on the immediacy of what you're lacking (money, health, happiness, or love), focus positively on the certainties of future abundance in all things. No goal is too big or too small. In identifying exactly what it is that you are trying to manifest, ask yourself some purposeful questions:

What is my specific goal?

Do I want a concrete object?

Do I want to change a behavior?

What is it I want to accomplish?

What do I want to feel? to do? to find?

What do I want to become? to experience?

If you're not clear on what it is exactly you are trying to manifest, how is the Universe supposed to fill your order? Throughout this and upcoming chapters, I use the word *order* to mean *thought*. Placing Your Order really means Placing Your Thoughts to manifest. But. use whatever you feel most comfortable in using that rings true for you.

Specific vs. Nonspecific Orders (Thoughts)

Both specific and nonspecific orders work well. Just how specific or nonspecific you should be about your Intent depends upon what you're manifesting. It's actually fun to build upon your Intent so you can get JUST EXACTLY what you want. The more specific you are about what it is you really want, the more likely you're going to get exactly what you ordered. But how many times have you thought you wanted something but when you got it, it wasn't what you thought you wanted. That's why I normally prefer the nonspecific or *perfect* order. I'll explain what I mean a little later in this chapter.

Specific Orders

Let's start with something specific and simple, for example, wanting a concrete object, because manifesting objects are pretty easy. I like to place a specific order when I am absolutely sure of what it is I want. Okay, so

---

here's my specific Intent: "I want to buy a new dress for the upcoming company Christmas party." Seems pretty straight forward.

You can be even more specific because you have a specific amount of money to spend and you (think) you know exactly what you're looking for: that lovely green velvet dress, just below the knees, size 12, for $150 that makes you look great, and fits comfortably.

In addition, since you hate last minute shopping, you want to add something about the timing so that you can enjoy the shopping experience. Your Intent is now: "I want to buy a lovely green velvet dress, just below the knees, size 12, for not more than $150, that fits me well, is comfortable, and makes me look great, in plenty of time for the upcoming company Christmas party so that I can enjoy this shopping experience." Whew! Now this is an excellent order. It's very specific and you've covered all the bases that are important to you. Or so you think!

Specific Order Downfalls
A major downfall in why our specific orders don't manifest is that we start to change our order. Instead of that lovely green dress, below the knees, velvet, size 12, for $150, we begin to change our minds: "What I really want is an above-the-knee, black cocktail dress for no more than $100." And so we place our order (again)...

Oops, then we decide (again) "What I really want is a sequined pants suit for \$125." Can you see the problem?

The Universe is unclear about what it is you really want. Each thought not only negates the previous order, but by changing your order, the intensity of your desire changes and so the final order lacks the emotional impetus required. The final result is that nothing gets manifested. There are no "trade-ins and no refunds" when stating our Intent!

Even when you are specific and you're REALLY sure of what you want, since we are only human, we can sometimes leave important things out of our order. For example, I had been suffering from the heat while riding on the metro to work each morning. I wanted a fan. I mean I REALLY wanted and needed a fan. Since I knew what I wanted, my order was: "My Intent is to have a fan that is pretty, small enough to fit into my purse, large enough to really cool me down, and of course, it has to be inexpensive!" That weekend, I went to a flea market with my friend, something I had never done before. As we were getting ready to leave the flea market, I took a last stroll down one of the aisles and sure enough, there was a lovely fan, just the right size and only cost me \$1.00. Needless to say, I was very pleased with myself and my ability to manifest. It couldn't have been more than one week later that my manifested fan broke while on the metro. Guess I should have mentioned something about wanting a sturdy fan as well! Do you see what I mean about covering all your bases? It's tough because, after all, we're only human and can't encompass everything we want our manifestation to be when using a specific order.

Nonspecific (Perfect) Orders

When you use a nonspecific order, what you're really doing is providing an outline of your Intent and then giving it over to the Universe. I also refer to this as the perfect order. Why? Because I know and believe that God truly knows what I want (and need). He looks into the deepest part of my heart and soul and provides me with the manifestation which is perfect for me.

Let's continue with the example of buying a new dress, but this time using a nonspecific order. If you're like me, you shop under the motto, "I'll know it when I see it." All I DO know is that I need something new to wear for an upcoming event. Using the same Intent of manifesting an outfit for an upcoming event, but not having specific details, I change my Intent: "I want to buy an outfit for my upcoming company Christmas party that fits me well, is comfortable, and makes me look great, in plenty of time for the upcoming company Christmas party so that I can enjoy this shopping experience." This is the first part

---

of the nonspecific order. I know it does sound pretty specific, but notice I haven't mentioned anything about the type, color, style or cost. Now, having learned that I might actually not know EVERY circumstance regarding something I'm trying to manifest (remember that fan?), I add the phrase: "...or the equivalent that is right and perfect for me." It's called the Law of Equivalency. It lets you cover all your bases. So now, my new Intent is: "I want to buy an outfit for my company's upcoming Christmas party, or the equivalent that is right and perfect for me, that fits me well, is comfortable, and makes me look great, in plenty of time for the party so that I can enjoy this shopping experience." How many times have we all gone out shopping for something we think we know we are looking for, only to find something totally different that works so much better?

This is why I generally prefer to use the perfect order in most of my manifestations. I have found that whenever I leave it to God to tweak or fine tune my order, it comes back to me better than I could have ever imagined. We're only human so we don't know what we truly want or how what we truly want will affect ourselves or others, but God does. God has taken into account, not only how my order will affect me, but makes sure my manifestation is for the highest good and greatest joy for all.

Combination of Specific AND Nonspecific Orders
Sometimes, I like to use a combination of both the specific and nonspecific (perfect) types of order. Because, believe it or not, I do have specific wants or needs filled when I place an order. For example, I'm looking to buy a new house.

Here's the specific part of my Intent which I MUST have: "I want a beautiful new home on the beach with 5 bedrooms, 4 baths, a family room, with balconies that go around the entire house. It must be open and airy, with lots of light; and everyone who steps foot into my home must feel positive, loving vibrations. I want to be able to look out and see the ocean from the front and sides of my house and trees out of the back of my house."

Okay, this does sound pretty specific! But I've really only put in my manifestation that which I really know I want. I know there are so many other variables in finding my perfect beach home. So here's where the nonspecific phrase "or the equivalent, that is right and perfect for me," should be used (here's where I'm leaving it up to God to fine tune my order for the reasons mentioned previously). While my Intent remains the same, I add "or, the equivalent that is right and perfect for me." I can now take a deep breath and know, really know that my order is making its way to me.

Using the Right Verb

Verbs are incredibly important in structuring your order. Having, being, doing, feeling, finding, and experiencing are very, very different verbs and will most definitely color your manifestation. Let me give you an example. I was going down to the Keys in Florida and wanted to find a specific brand of sunglasses. So, I placed my order with the Intent: "I want to find sunglasses like the ones I got in Paris all those years ago, or the equivalent that is perfect for me." (Here I used a combination of specific and nonspecific). Guess what? I found them in a place where normally we wouldn't have even gone into. We had driven in the wrong direction and were making a U-turn when I spotted this little shop. We went in and, lo and behold, there they were! I was so jazzed. But guess what? I didn't have enough money! I had FOUND the sunglasses alright, but oops...guess I should have put something in there about having the resources to actually buy them! I now add as part of every Intent, "I now have the required resources available to obtain that which I am manifesting." It's important to note that resources can be anything...money, time, experience, people, etc.

In using the first example for Intent, it now changes to: "I want to buy an outfit for my upcoming company Christmas party that fits me well, is comfortable, and makes me look great, in plenty of time for the party, and I can enjoy this shopping experience, or the equivalent that is right and perfect for me, with the required resources available to obtain that which I am manifesting."

Using the Right Tense
Not only is the right verb required, but the right tense is **mandatory**. In fact, it's **critical**. Your request must take the present tense of the verb, as if you already have that which you are ordering. This is a very intriguing concept and it took me some time to wrap my mind around it.

Here's what you're doing when you say the object you desire is already yours. You are forming the energy channel connection, which establishes, in the Now, the relationship or linkage between yourself and the object you desire. The relationship between you and your intended object becomes the IS, the present tense of the verb. The very word 'is' establishes this energy connection. And so, your desired object manifests in your presence at the right time and at the right place. It is just making its' way to you, just as you are making your way to it. At the right time (remember God's perfect timing?) the two meet. I firmly believe that if I take that positive attitude that "it's a done deal," then no doubt can enter into my thoughts.

———

Timing: Deadlines vs. Open-Ended Requests

The point of being able to manifest what we want when we need it is what this book is all about. Otherwise, what's the point? The purpose of being able to manifest is so we can meet our needs, whatever they are and whenever they arise.

Deadline orders are usually very serious manifestations. They are fraught with emotion and usually with a feeling of being overwhelmed by current circumstances: "My rent is due next month. I don't have the money to pay it, and I can't see anyway I'm going to have it." Or, "My children are returning to school and need clothes and supplies, but I'm strapped for cash." Here's where unconditional belief comes into play (we'll discuss this more fully in the chapter on Belief). A deadline order requires the deepest desire as well as unconditional belief in order for it to become a successful manifestation. Having faith is anything but easy, but it is an unconditional requirement with these types of orders. These manifestations are placed with the following Intent: "I am able to pay next month's rent on time because I now have the required resources available" or "I am now able to purchase clothes and supplies for my children in plenty of time before school starts because I now have the required resources available." Please notice I didn't include "or the equivalent that is right and perfect for me" because hard cash (as the resource) was the required Intent.

Open-ended orders are great when there is no urgency for the order manifesting within a certain time period. They can be either specific or nonspecific (perfect) or a combination of the two. It's a lot easier to practice your manifestation abilities when the necessity is still real, but not frantic. And it is in open-ended orders that we should definitely use the "that or something equivalent that is right and perfect for me" as part of the Intent.

Visualizations

Sometimes it's advantageous when you start learning to manifest that you use some sort of visualization that helps you feel you've placed your order. Speaking the words sometimes don't seem enough, especially to a beginner. The use of visualizations can really assist you. It took me a while to come up with something because, while I'm definitely a feeler, I didn't consider myself a visualizer. And because I believed that, I couldn't visualize. (Our thoughts create our reality, remember?) Once I realized I can do whatever I think I can do, I then applied what I learned. The mantra I now use for visualizing is: "I know I can visualize exactly the way I need to place my order."

Another good visualization is seeing your thought as a mold, which I used in the earlier chapter. Picture the car, house, or whatever it is you want to manifest as a mold into which this vibrating energy is being poured and which will be transformed into the shape in which you've placed your order. Or, the energy can be like a cookie cutter, imprinting the form of your thought into this creative fabric of the Universe. The main point is to use whatever visualization method works for you!!

Now, whenever I place an order, I use the concept of a blackboard. The vibrating energy is my blackboard. It soaks up my writing, and through its plasticity, my order becomes manifested. I like to use the following picture: I see a beautiful blackboard, so big it encompasses the entire screen of my vision, upon which I write my order. My blackboard is made up of black velvet, and it is the most beautiful one I can image. I begin to place my order. Coming out of my right index finger (because I'm right-handed) is sparkling gold ink. The ink flows effortlessly across the blackboard. I deliberately write each word in the most beautiful handwriting imaginable, feeling each word to my bones. When I'm done, I write "Thank You" and sign my full name. The moment I sign it, I visualize all the writing melting into the blackboard, and I know that the Universe has picked up my order!

By now, we've come to understand just how important Intent is in making sure we get what we want and why this is the first part of the equation. It forces us to think about just what it is we want (specific vs. nonspecific). We must state our order as if we already have possession of it by using the correct verb and tense, and not change our order in midstream. Using visualizations help us to place our order with confidence.

We're now ready to move to the second step required: Motive. The next important question we should ask ourselves is, "WHY do I want it?"

K.C. Craig

Motive
(Why do you want it?)
Equation: (I + Mo)

Be generous with your Motive and kind in your choices, for Motive is the foundation upon which your order is anchored. The strongest and most solid foundation is based upon the Motive of helping others while you are helping yourself achieve your desires.

Understanding your Motive is a time of soul searching. To discover your Motive, you have to stop and really ask yourself why you want to manifest this or that, and you MUST be honest with yourself because there's no fooling the Universe. Ask yourself, "Am I truly speaking from my loving heart and soul?"

Be Careful What You Order Up
You MUST be clear as to why you want to manifest. Do I want my good over the good of another? Is my Motive to intentionally hurt another? How will what I manifest affect others? It IS important to take the time to include others in your Motive because it causes you to stop and think just how what you want to manifest may affect others and helps clarify for yourself why it is you truly want it. Why? There's this little thing called the Law of Attraction, remember? Whatever you give out, you get

---

back! I like to think of the Law of Attraction as the Golden Rule. If you don't use the Golden Rule in placing your order, believe me you'll have only yourself to blame when the negative energy you sent out when you placed your order lands upon your doorstep.

The More the Merrier

One's manifestation can help others on so many levels. It's also very spiritually cost effective. Besides getting what YOU want, your Motive provides you with an opportunity to include others to help meet their needs as well. It becomes a very economical way of achieving the win/win scenario, which we all know God loves so well. "How can what I want be manifested in such a way that others will benefit as well; that it will be for the highest good and greatest joy for all?"

As an example, let's go back to the perfect home on the beach that I'm manifesting. So how are others included? Wouldn't it be great that we buy our home from someone who really wants or needs to sell it? And what about the person who really needs a commission sells it or the Feng Shui consultant whose gift of beauty and peach can be utilized and appreciated, or the contractor who needs the business...get the drift? I can make up at least a dozen reasons, if I take the time to see that my order can help so many others at the same time.

You don't HAVE to include others when you manifest. Your "me only" Motive does, indeed, manifest your desire just as assuredly. But why be so cheap with your Motive? Remember this: the creative energy of the Universe flows in the direction of the highest good for all. Because God loves to distribute creative energy efficiently, the She will funnel much more energy and more quickly into the "more the merrier" Motive that benefits the greatest number of beings!

Manifesting for Others

I often ask myself, "Should I manifest for others? How do I know that all my good intentions won't do them harm in some way I don't foresee? Why do I want to manifest this or that for another? Is it out of unconditional love for this soul? Or, do I have an ulterior Motive? How do I know what is right for them?" Let's face it. I don't know and neither do you. But God does. So when I'm manifesting for another, I use the perfect Intent order. I always ask that God provide them with their highest good and greatest joy, knowing it is always that by asking God to manifest for another, they will receive what's perfect for them.

Well, by now, I know what I want to manifest and why. You'll notice I've put a parenthesis around Intent and Motive in my equation. It's because I think of them in combination with each other. What I want and why I want it are two questions which just naturally fit together because how can you want something if you don't know why you want it? The next question I need to ask myself is "How MUCH do I want it?"

Desire
(How Much Do You Want It?)
Equation: $(I + Mo) + D^I$

During that one moment of placing your order, your Desire must be as intense and as vital to you as your Desire to take your next breath. Period. Otherwise, don't bother. Because, in effect, you are manifesting the effect of your emotions. Our most successful manifestations are directly proportional to the intensity of our emotions. This intensity is the momentum behind our Desires.

Desire and Intensity
Thoughts are so powerful, especially when they are based upon some intense emotion. Let's consider the words Desire and Intensity. Desire means longing for, yearning for, or hungering for. Intensity means power, depth, ardor, fervor, forcefulness, potency, zeal, passion, or emotion.

What are you longing for, yearning for, and hungering for? How passionate are you? What is the depth of your zeal to achieve what you want to manifest?

Being wishy-washy in wanting this or that is like tapping lightly on the door of the Universe, hoping our knock is heard and the door opens so we can place our order. Since the Intensity of our Desire is the power behind our manifestation reaching this creating vibrating energy, not

---

only does our Desire reach its' intended target, but the Intensity of our Desire propels our thoughts to smash through that door and drop it right in God's lap!!

We desire so many things throughout our lives. We all want lots and lots of things....but only those that I truly, emphatically wanted have come to me. I've found that without exception my most successful manifestations have been when I say I want something in a moment of Intense Desire or need, right to the depths of my soul. For example, as I am sweating on the Metro, you can believe me that the only thing I truly desire at that moment is a fan! And it is in that moment of Intense Desire that I've placed my order, whether or not I'm aware of it. I'm really good at manifesting emotional items. It is not until my Desire is so Intense that nothing else will do that I'm able to manifest most successfully.

We had the same furniture for the past 14 years. It didn't bother me because "it would do and we were at that time tight on money." (Let's not forget that I'm that immaterial girl in a material world!) Then, one day I was so uncomfortable on this lumpy, scratchy, ugly, old couch, I'd had enough (even for me) and put out into the Universe my Intense Desire for the perfect new, comfortable, and pleasant looking couch, knowing we had the resources to obtain it when we found I mean, I

REALLY wanted it. In that one moment, the Intensity of my Desire to have a new couch became as important to me as taking my next breath." Yep, you guessed it; we now have a wonderful new couch, perfect in every way. I left the "details" to God, but asked Him to include in the purchase of our couch to benefit others as well. Even if I don't know how they benefited, by including others in my request, I know they were. That's how God works.

Now that we know the Intensity of our Desire is vital for a successful thought manifestation, we are ready to explore the final step. And it's a kicker…Belief. The final question: Do I BELIEVE it's mine?

Belief
(Doubt is Out!)
Equation: $(I + Mo) + D^I + B$

Whatever you believe is possible, IS. Whatever you believe isn't, ISN'T. This means that whatever you believe is possible can become real, right here and now. The other side of the coin is that whatever you believe is not possible has no hope of becoming real for you. Believing is, by far, the most complex, yet a most critical aspect of a successful manifestation. Until now, I never really understood the saying, "It is done unto you as you believe." But the power of Belief is incredible in changing your life into whatever you Believe it is or should be.

Believing (Faith/Knowing)
Doubt is out! Eliminate it now! **Belief means implicit, unconditional faith and certain unequivocal knowing and trusting that your manifestation is making its way to you, just as you are making your way to it.** And, with God's perfect timing, you meet. To really "know," you must have the maximum intensity of Belief. I ask myself, "Am I truly *beleezing*? [Belief + is, and it's pronounced as be-leez-ing.]. It reminds me to ask myself if I believe in my heart and soul what I want to manifest is already mine. It is vital that you believe what you are

---

speaking; otherwise, forget about manifesting anything and save your breath!

Practice, practice, and practice until you KNOW, really KNOW that what you have asked for is already yours. But how do you really know? How do you truly beleeze? What can you do to help you learn to beleeze? These are perhaps the toughest questions that we've asked ourselves up to now.

Mantras (Affirmations)

I like to use Mantras to help me shift my thinking and change my thoughts into knowing and beleezing my manifestation is here and now...first on a conscious level, until my new thoughts can manifest on the subconscious level. Then, from this subconscious level, my thoughts now somehow feel real to me, and I believe in them. It's really an amazing process. And once the subconscious and conscious levels are united in Belief, watch out; for what you are ordering will most surely be yours!

What is a Mantra? The word *Mantra* is originally from the Sanskrit language where it is considered as religious or mystical syllables used by devotee students to help them to focus their thoughts and concentrate inwardly, until they reach a point of complete stillness within. The word *Aum* is an excellent example. I like to think of a Mantra as a mechanical way of convincing myself of a truth, a reality not yet realized, through the repetition of positive statements (*Affirmations*). For the purpose of this book, I use the word "Mantra" as a way of focusing my thoughts and energy on manifesting a specific concept or idea. How does the repetition of a Mantra or an Affirmation help you truly believe? Well, they work on the conscious level first. Whenever you repeat an affirmation, it lifts your conscious thoughts to a whole different level of vibration. What you're doing is immersing or flooding your consciousness with the affirmation in such a way that it can only think of this as real. I don't know how this works, I only know that it indeed does work, like a charm.

It takes repeating and repeating and repeating the Mantra or Affirmation until it becomes a part of you. This is how it worked for me. The first Mantra I ever used, I still use today...except now it has become a part of my entire being and way of thinking, "Everything is working for good." I can't tell you how many times a day I used to say this Mantra, even though in the beginning, they were just words to me. Then, the more and more I said them, the more and more I began to feel comfortable with the words...until one day, this Mantra became my Belief and my Belief became a part of me...and I truly beleezed it to be so. At that point, I started to see that the events of my life were working out just as I believed, even though at the time, it might not have seemed like it.

As I matured in my thinking through the years, I've now added: "for the highest good and greatest joy for all." I think that as we grow spiritually, we naturally want to include others in our manifestations, because it's the awareness that we are not the only ones involved when we manifest something. I've since included "in my conscious mind, in my subconscious mind, and in Universal Mind," because these are the levels upon which Manifesting takes place. I now know and beleeze to the depths of my being that "In my conscious mind, in my subconscious mind, and in Universal Mind, everything is working for the highest good and greatest joy for all." Give it try and you'll be amazed at your results. Let me just say, ONE MORE TIME, practice, practice, practice!!

For two years I was in a situation that was unbearable. The absolute worst professional experience I've ever had. And through it all, I just kept repeating my Mantra, "Everything is working for the highest good and greatest joy of all." When my time in professional Hell was over, I had a chance to reflect and see the many positive aspects which came out of this experience. It actually WAS for my highest good and the outcome DID become a great joy for me. This is how powerful the right Mantra for you can be.

Only you can know which Mantra works for you. You'll automatically know because you will discover that it becomes a part of your essence, your being, and then, a part of your absolute Belief. Once you have absolute Belief, the manifestation is yours!

Mantra vs. Intent

Perhaps some clarity is now needed between what we mean by what is your Intent vs. what is your Mantra. Don't get confused between what the Intent part of your order is with what your Mantra is **for** that order. They are two completely different concepts. Mantras or Affirmations are used only **after** you've placed your order. Your Mantra is not your specific Intent. It is merely a device you use to help yourself really beleeze that your order is a done deal! It assists your Belief part of the order. You've already placed your order. Remember my Intent for that beach house? It is quite lengthy and involved, which often Intents are. However, my Mantra for that beach house order is short and sweet, "In my conscious mind, in my subconscious mind and in Universal Mind, the perfect beach house is making its way to me as I am making my way to it, for the highest good and greatest joy for all." I don't need to reiterate my complete Intent. That's not the function of a Mantra. The reason I suggest keeping your Mantra brief is that you're going to be repeating it over and over and over again:

while you're brushing your teeth, or while you're getting dressed, or while you're in line for that cup of coffee. The KISS principle, "Keep it simple, stupid," says it all.

So, go have some fun and play with Mantras. They can be for health, wealth, happiness, friends, employment, love...whatever you want. That's what's so cool about Mantras. I'm now working on another Mantra: "In my conscious mind, in my subconscious mind and in Universal Mind, together, Richard and I are fabulously wealthy, phenomenally healthy, and ecstatically happy, for the highest good and greatest joy for all." Just imagine the outcome when this Mantra finally becomes as true and real for me as the sun I see rising in the morning!

Belief through Action
Belief through Action; Action through Belief: Become proactive when required. This shows the Universe that you DO believe that your order has been filled. In life, that which is most important requires action on our part in some way or another. We are in partnership with the Universe and must contribute to this partnership. You've noticed that throughout the book, I've used the phrase "making its way to you just as you are making your way to it." It's part of this partnership. This means that you aren't just sitting around and waiting for God to fill your order. No, indeed. You are doing whatever you need to do

as your part in this manifesting process. I'm sure you've all heard of the adage, "You can't win the lottery unless you buy the ticket!" I know that's simplistic, but the concept is just the same. Belief through action. For example, let's say you want to manifest becoming a doctor. Your Mantra or Affirmation is "I know I am a great doctor; my skills are being used for the highest and greatest good for all." Your part of the "Action through Belief" is that you're going to have to graduate from college, go to medical school, and do an internship and a residency before you become a doctor. You're not going to become a doctor by sitting on the couch watching TV and munching chips. But you ARE going to become a great doctor…that's already a given, because you know that you're going to have to take the action required to get there. Can you see the concept I'm trying to relay to you? Let's give you another example. "I have perfect health." But if I continue to eat improperly, do not exercise, or get enough sleep, how am I going to manifest perfect health? Remember that this is a partnership with the Universal Mind. Do your part, and God will do Hers.

Cultural or Social Beliefs
Besides having to come to terms with your own Beliefs, you'll need to check to see if any of those Beliefs are really yours or if they are really part of "cultural or social" Belief. It's important to know which Beliefs are yours

and which Beliefs belong to a group of which you are a part, for example, humanity! These types of Beliefs are usually generalities that have become a part of your subconscious Belief system as being universally true. "As you age, you're not as active as when you were younger," "There is so much wrong with the world, there's nothing I can do to help," "War is inevitable," or a million other Beliefs which belong not to you, but to your tribe, or your culture, or the society in which you live!

An Atmosphere of Expecting and Accepting
In addition to beleezing, you MUST surround yourself in a spiritual atmosphere of expectancy and complete acceptance, **knowing** your manifestation is making its way to you, because it can do nothing else! Since the word "spiritual" has a different connotation for each of us, you may need to try different things to transform your current doubting atmosphere. When I feel I'm not really in that beleezing mode, I've found that music helps me change my vibrational energy, which lifts me and my feelings into true beleezing.

When we provide this atmosphere of expectancy, we are really saying to God, "Yep, I beleeze it's on its way." Accepting says to the Universe: "I am worth the good that I am manifesting," "I am good enough, and I deserve it." I mention this because how many of us want something, but within ourselves, we do not feel we are worthy enough? Usually, our lack of believing in our worthiness comes from some old mind tape we have been playing all our lives. Whether it comes from disapproving parents, friends, or situations in life, they all have built up this idea of "not being good enough." *We don't have to be smart, or pretty, or powerful to be able to manifest.* We already know that we are empowered by God to be creative, just because we are living, breathing beings.

Let Go, Let God
"Letting go and letting God" are more than just words. It's a concept which is immensely powerful, yet difficult to do. Why? It is very difficult to do because it's human nature to think of our wants and needs even after having gone through the various steps in manifesting. We hold on to our order with all our might, because if we were to let it go, what would we have to hold on to? And here's where we get into trouble. I know it sounds easy to let go....but it's anything but easy! How do you stop thinking about it? I try to shift my focus onto other things and give it truly over to God. "Letting God" most certainly speaks to the notion that God can do it far better than we've thought. God takes our order, looks inside our heart, and manifests our soul's desire better than our mere mortal minds are capable of conceiving. And don't forget this:

God is the timekeeper...when and where is up to Him. It allows me to just relax with my order...I just love that part!

It all goes back to the concept of what is perfect. We are finite human beings, and our ability to conceive of all angles and outcomes of that which we desire is limited, extremely limited. Limited in the following ways:

Do we really know what our highest good and greatest joy are?

Do we really know how what we are manifesting will affect others?

All we know is that we don't truly know! Our job is merely to place our order using the correct steps. It is the Universal Mind's responsibility to pick up the ball and run with it. You'll find your most successful manifestations are directly proportional to how much you can let go and let God. Don't give up! Just because you've placed your order with true beleezing, and it hasn't manifested yet, take heart. The ways and the means in which your manifestation exist lie in the power of God. It's not your job. Your job is to accept, take action, expect, believe, and know it is on its way.

Thank You

Have a grateful heart. Whenever I place an order, my final thoughts and words are ones of complete gratitude. In expressing our gratitude, we are sharing our joy and Belief in God's love and Her gift to us of this Universal Law of Cause and Effect...knowing that whatever comes is for the highest good and greatest joy for all. Really feel the joy that comes with being thankful. It's a blast.

Manifesting your order takes true beleezing, true faith. Saying Mantras or Affirmations will help you shift your consciousness and subconscious minds until they are united in your feeling of Belief that what you are saying makes it so. In an atmosphere of expectancy and acceptance, and taking action towards accomplishing that which you want manifested will help you move toward your manifestation. And when you finally let go, let God, you can relax and know that your order indeed has been placed...better than you can even imagine.

Remember: You've already established the IS relationship in the Now with that which you desire through your thoughts. When you beleeze that which is desired already is, accept it as fact. It is this acknowledgement that causes your order to become successfully filled.

Now, let's proceed to see what we've manifested.

MANIFESTATION
(Voila! Here it is!)
Equation: $(I + Mo) + D^1 + B = M$

Well, you've placed your order…but remember, you must be receptive to that which you will be served! The order you've placed (your thought) is based upon your past experiences, and you can only imagine that of which you have already experienced or have knowledge. Yet, you MAY be served something you never had before imagined when you allow God fill your order. That's what happens when you let go, let God. Take heart and be happy because what has been manifested has come from the Infinite Mind, and whatever is served is for the highest good and greatest joy for all. E-x-c-e-l-l-e-n-t.

Manifesting through the power of our thoughts and free will are tremendous tools that we have been given by God to create our own happiness or our own sorrow. I don't know about you, but I feel incredibly empowered, knowing the power to create my reality lies within me and me alone. Will I accept my authorship? You bet. Am I willing to accept my responsibility for creating my world? Absolutely. Why? Well, I know I've correctly used the steps required of Intention, Motive, Desire, and Belief to produce my heart's desire. I know what I want, why I want it, how much I want it, and I have an absolute, unconditional belief it is already mine.

We've learned that you must know what you want…what is your Intention? To get the most "bang for my buck," I ask myself, "How can I align my Intention with God's Intention, my Motive with God's Motive of creating the highest good and greatest joy for all…achieving that win/win scenario for all involved?" "Does my Desire for this Intention evoke in me such a passion that nothing else will do?" "Do I already accept, beleeze, and know that which I desire is already making its way to me just as I am making my way to it?" "Have I let go and let God take the reins?"

And, don't forget to always ask yourself: "What does true happiness mean to me?" It will, of course, be different for all of us. Sure, material goodies make us happy, but once you've attained the material prosperity you desire, will you be happy? I ask because you will still be you, regardless of whether or not you can live anywhere you want to live, do anything you want to do, or have anything you want to have. Manifesting forces us to take a good hard look at ourselves. For me, I have found that peace of mind, physical health, a loving heart, and the privilege of being of service are my sincerest and truest desires. What are yours?

It is my sincerest wish that by now, you've had your "*aha*" moment I mentioned in the beginning of the book;

that by understanding the steps which make up a successful manifestation, you are now clear in the understanding that you are the creator of your life and your reality.

Go and have fun in exploring yourself and in finding what you truly want to have, to do, and to become. Your heart's desire is but a thought away.

May the God in me
Meet and greet the God in you.
And in that moment,
We are one with humanity;
For I am in you,
And you are in me.

Notes

Notes

Notes

www.ingramcontent.com/pod-product-compliance
Lightning Source LLC
Chambersburg PA
CBHW071634040426
42452CB00009B/1613